SUBANIMAL YELLS

Subanimal yells,
Screaming to be heard,
Spewing out venom,
Through the literary word,
Subversive, sullen expression,
Neither drink nor drug induced
Just an average individual,
trying to tell the truth.

INTRODUCTION

I was brought up in a rough world of uncertainty, where survival was an achievement—stability an added bonus and a sense of humour essential. I wasn't born to be creative.
I wrote these poems over the space of a year during 1982/83. My inspiration was pure frustration and anger. I drew from hard experience. When I say I am a street poet—you'd better believe it!
I was born in Nottingham in 1957. My father, who was totally blind, did a variety of jobs including baking, cobbling and G.P.O. switchboard operating. My mother, when she was well enough, was an infants teacher and also a secretary. She was one of the working class women who received a scholarship after the war. I had two older sisters. My younger brother, I first met when I was six. I don't remember much of Nottingham as we were always on the move, looking for somewhere to live. Suprisingly, I still have a faint Midlands accent.
I was first taken into care at the age of four with my sisters. The family had been living a caravan site in Brighton because private landlords did not like children adding yet more marks to their inferior properties. I recall being a very small person in a frightening world of strange adults who's sole purpose in life was to make me eat my greens!
After two years, the family were given a council house in Ilford. This was the first time that we had been together as a family for any length of time.
As a child, I found my mother's illness confusing and frightening. It seemed to run in a constant cycle and I got to know each phase. I used to look forward to the periods of remission which took longer to arrive over the years. The word 'Schizophrenia' was frequently bandied about. I didn't know what it meant—except that my mum was one. Mum often couldn't cope at home, consequently I was ridiculed at school for being scruffy. School was never a regular thing as mum didn't usually wake up too early.
Violent arguments between my parents often erupted into fights which usually ended with the police being called and my mum being taken to the local psychiatric hospital. It was a place I was obliged to visit but never liked to. I learnt words like 'whore' and 'bastard' at a very tender age.
At the age of nine, I found myself in Dr Barnardoes. Everybody assumed that I had no parents so I couldn't understand why I was there. Perhaps my parents wanted me adopted?
It was at the age of eleven that my oldest sister introduced me to shop-lifting. We both got caught and I was sent to an Assessment centre and was put on a Supervision Order until the age of eighteen.
I learnt to become "harder" and rougher than the other kids there in order to get attention. The result was trouble and more trouble. I played truant constantly, got involved in fights and ran away at every opportunity. I became an "uncontrollable problem". From then I seemed to be in and out of care in various institutions. I felt like a yoyo—I felt confused and let down by everyone concerned. I counted that I had been put in care sixteen times. There was nothing stable in my life. At the age of sixteen everybody's problems were solved—except mine. School advised me to leave without taking any 'O' levels and the Social Services decided I was too old to be in care. Suddenly my future was placed into my hands. I came out of my corner, battle scarred but fighting!
Mum became permanently ill. She often took to the bottle during a depression but now she was definately an alchoholic. I went through a succession of office jobs but I became bored very quickly and at my wits end with the pressures at home. Dad's chronic bronchitis was getting progressively worse.

Late in 1976 I heard a record which knocked me sideways. It was "Anarchy in the UK" by the Sex Pistols. I began to check out the scene which was emerging in London. By the enlightened it was called a 'revolutionary youth culture'. The sensationalist daily papers coined the phrase 'Punk Rock'.

Mark P., an ordinary lad from Deptford had been writing his own fanzine for some time. It was a creative and useful alternative to the national, capitalist 'Rock Press'. "Sniffin Glue" became my bible till I got myself together enough to start *my* fanzine 'Apathy in Ilford'. I couldn't believe how easy it was to write and put forward my ideas. I also wrote articles for 'Rock against Racism' which I became involved with.

After just six months, the scene became a parody of itself. Bands sold out to big business, people began to buy their clothes instead of making them. "Punk" became tame and respectable. Those of us who believed in the original ideas and meanings left, disillusioned, saddened and worst of all, beaten.

In 1978 my father died of emphysema. At the age of 21 I decided to become a nurse. I was lucky enough to become part of the rowdiest SEN training set my local hospital had every known. We were an embarrasment to our school, tolerated by the Ward Sisters and encouraged by the Doctors! Most of us passed our exams but not many of us studied very much. I loved it on the wards. I understood human suffering and felt I could relate well to my patients. Nobody could accuse me of being patronsing!

During this time my eldest sister took an overdose and threw herself in the river Thames. They dragged her out of there after about a week. I felt numbed by her death—I still do. I have felt like giving up on life many times but I'm still here surviving.

Whe I qualified as a nurse in 1981 I didn't know what to do next. I had always been interested in the field of orthopaedics. When I was accepted to do a year's training in orthopaedics at Northampton I thought I had done a good thing. Never had I regretted a decision so much as this one. Everybody up there seemed so reactionary and out of touch with reality. The hospital left a lot to be desired and the town was half dead. I examined my past 3 years of existence and found that I had become very apathetic.

The Healthworkers strikes had begun and everyone around me seemed oblivious to the decline of the NHS. They wanted a decent living wage, adequate care for their patients but did not want to stand up and fight for these basic rights. The hierarchical nursing structure was becoming a bitter pill to swallow. I began to feel my identity as a person was being denied. Every time I tried to assert my personality and say "I refuse to be a nonentity, I won't be absorbed nor lose my power to think", I was put down. I began to write about my feelings past and present. Poems just seemed to evolve effortlessly. The only person I showed them to was Pauline, my sister. She urged me to keep them which I did. In 1983 I approached Centerprise with a view to publication. They mean a lot to me and I hope will be understood by those who read them. I hope it gives encouragement to other working class writers who have been lead to believe that the ability to write and create is a middle class privilege. Go home and create something entirely new!

Sharon Dunham
February 1984

THIS BOOK IS DEDICATED TO:-

Pauline and Ade, who mean more to me than mere brother and sister. Veronica, who didn't live long enough for me to show that I cared.
My parents, who despite everything always encouraged me to think.
A man from Northampton who I can't name but still care about.
Lastly. To people who underestimated me as a person and made this book possible.

THE BIG LIGHT

Someone turned the light out,
Everybody panicked,
But I wasn't scared,
I saw it coming,
A long time ago.

MECHANICAL BREAKDOWN

I am the product,
You advertise,
I eat the garbage,
You feed the lies
Racism, Fascism, Sexism
You try to rationalise.
But its a product that,
I won't buy.
Something got stuck
In the machinery,
Something jerked my,
Social conscience
You underestimated
My powers of observation
And now my apathy,
Has turned to agitation.

SUPPRESSION

When was the last time,
That I cried?
I can't remember,
It was so long ago,
I'm not devoid of emotion,
So why can't I show it?
I channel my hurt,
Into anger,
And turn people away,
It churns up inside me,
My brain explodes,
But I can't share my pain,
So nobody knows.

DOLEFUL EYES

For the eternal school leavers

I'm 18 years of age,
Already over the hill,
Give me a job, some respect,
And some money in my hand,
Don't give me excuses,
I'm not a statistic
Or a leper to be shunned,
You won't break me you bastards!

NORTHAMPTON FRIDAY NIGHT

Deadtown!
Where the sane lives in asylums,
And the insane fight in pubs,
Downtown Northampton Friday night,
Where an accidental step,
On a protruding foot,
Could end up in a fight,
The highlight of the week,
Is a grope behind the bus shelter,
And a spew on the last bus home,
Downtown Northampton,
Where boredom breeds insanity.

THE BEAT THAT DOESN'T CHANGE

Sleazy disco night clubs.
Where men undress you,
With their beery eyes,
You came to dance?
No chance!
Are you having fun?
Are you going to be the one,
Who's being had tonight?
the record doesn't change,
Everynight's the same,
And it really is a shame,
That people have to,
Live like this.

GHETTO BLASTING

Sitting on a tube train,
Armed with my ghetto blaster,
The revolutionary sounds,
Getting louder, getting faster.
An art rat shakes his trendy head,
A tired punk shakes his leg,
A black kid starts to bodypop,
A city gent starts to see red,
Makes for the door in a wild frenzy
The power I hold in my batteries,
Makes me feel strong,
Bringing music to the streets,
Is that what Malcolm McLaren said?

PASS THE SPLIFF

Pass the spliff,
Let me nullify my tired brain,
Taking in the soothing, pounding
Reggae music,
The Ethiopian dream,
Which I don't share,
But it helps me cope with,
This constant down pressure,
Which is half killing me.

LE POSEURS

Took a bus to Camden Town,
Had my hair cut,
Walked around,
Trendy people, trendy clothes,
Come to Camden for the pose.

MARRIAGE

Marriage!
The ultimate a girl can aspire to
The age of sexual revolution?
You're still expected to say 'I do'
Teenage years wasted,
Looking for Mr. Right,
And when he eventually arrives
It should come as no suprise
To find he is boringly normal.
The age of feminism?
You're still expected to "Do right by him"
Iron his shirts,
Cook his meals, make the tea,
Tidy the house,
"Be nice" to him in bed.
Marriage,
The ultimate a girl can
Aspire to.

DROWNING IN VALIUM

Doctors dole out,
Depression lifting pills
Label people as mentally ill,
They don't have time,
To isolate the problem,
And a suicide statistic,
Is a pharmacuetical failure.

LIP SERVICE

I'll dance to your tune,
Whilst you hold the power.
You control my actions,
Monitor reactions
But you can't control my thoughts
I'm only paying lip service
Till my time comes,
As I know it must
Then I'll cut my strings,
And do to you,
What you did to me,
Did I detect a shudder?

MAGGIE'S FINGER

Maggie's got her finger on the button
Its trembling with excitement,
She just can't wait,
But first she has to make sure,
Her bunkers' ultra safe,
In her head she's made a date,
Till then, she'll just content herself,
With smashing the welfare state.

COLIN ROACH

Down at Stoke Newington nick,
Beneath the grimey streets,
There are rabbit hutches,
They call custody cells,
In these cells,
There are walls,
On these walls,
Are written names and slogans,
Mostly in scratchmarks,
One name is written in blood,
It is the name of Colin Roach,
And because it is written in blood
It can easily be erased,
. . . . just like his murder.

TACTICS

Out on the edge
I'm waiting.
I can't sit on the fence,
Where its neutral and negative.
I have to state my position
I can't be categorised,
Labelled and dispatched,
The best form of defence,
Is always attack.

BRIXTON CRISIS

Violence bursting onto the Brixton Street
Don't pity the policeman,
He chose his own destiny.
A dread picks up a brick,
And hurls it with a force,
Born of 400 years frustration
And we all look on,
And the blind politicians,
Ask what went wrong?
And the blood runs freely,
Down Railton Road,
And we all hear the question,
Its the answer we know,
The blind will never understand.

RUNNING

I ran away from home,
When I was four years old,
I was always running away.
When I was in care,
I ran to my parents,
Or to the country,
When I was at home,
I ran to the kid's homes,
Or to the police
Pleading with them,
To put me in care.
I ran from school —
I felt trapped
Now I'm an adult,
I run away
From my responsibilities,
Although I try not to.

UNCERTAINTY

In the early hours,
I was lying next to you,
I was awake,
I watched you sleeping,
You looked so peaceful,
I reached over and touched,
You soft black skin,
You opened you eyes,
Smiled and turned over,
I'm not really sure,
If you were pleased to see me.

LEFT HOLDING THE BLEEP

I was on call,
I didn't know it,
I thought you could see me,
Intelligent, articulate.
You only saw through me,
Available, convenient.
Isn't it strange?
Physical contact,
So intimate and personal,
Can be turned into,
Nothingness.
You should feel lucky,
That I graced you,
With my presence.

GENDER STEREOTYPE

If you take me home tonight
Am I under obligation?
If I don't want to sleep with you,
Will you leave me at the station?
Don't use my body,
I'm not an alleycat,
Won't get caught like a fly,
In your sexist spiders trap.

EXTERIOR GLOSS (2 COATS)

My aggressive stance,
Is only a protective device,
It takes a person,
With a degree of perception,
To cut through the framework
And realise —

I don't know why,
I want to alienate you,
I don't know why,
I want you to hate me,
Perhaps its my own insecurity.

HAPPY MOTHERS DAY

In a drunken stupor,
My mother said to me,
"You should have been stillborn"
Thank you mum,
Now I understand,
The meaning of true love,
The cord has been cut,
Years of anguish erased,
And now I shall never,
Have to see you again.

ASSESSMENT CENTRE

When I was a kid,
They put me in an assessment centre
I learnt to swear,
I learnt to steal,
I learnt to become,
What they thought I was.
But throughout my re-shaping,
They couldn't take away,
My intelligence.
I learnt to use my wit,
I used my cunning instincts
I learnt to assess
Those who were assessing me
And in the end,
I came out un-tainted.

IDENTITY CRISIS

I succumbed to the temptation,
Of becoming a non entity,
I played the game,
And towed the line,
Till it became too much for me,
I began to feel alienated,
I was losing the real me,
So like a reptile,
I shed my skin,
And managed to set myself free.

SEEING IS BELIEVING

I never believed in,
Fairy stories
Childhood innocence was,
Smashed out of me,
Before I even learnt to read
I knew about violence,
Irrational behaviour,
Emotional blackmail,
And inverted snobbery,
But now I'm older,
I feel pity,
For people who cannot,
Read through the lines,
For people who live a,
Sheltered life,
I listen, I look,
And then transcend.

NATIONAL PRIDE

When I was a baby,
They stuck a union jack in my hand
Drove it in so deep,
that it took years of determination,
To get rid of a foreign body,
Which I never asked for,
The great British inheritance,
Which people keep rooted in them,
Out of complacency and ignorance.

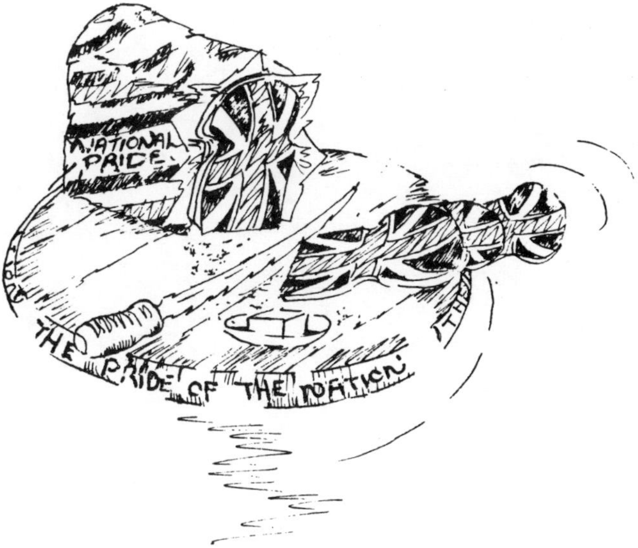

MY FRIENDS

My friends say
I should be satisfied,
My friends say,
I should feel lucky,
My friends say,
I've got a chip on my shoulder,
My friends say,
I shouldn't knock the system,
My friends are,
Happy in their ignorance,
My friends are,
Conditioned and contented,
My friends don't,
Understand my anger,
My friends don't live in
Innercity squalor,
My friends are,
Still my friends.

IN A MILITANT STYLE

Feel the heat,
Down on the street,
Move your feet,
Better check the beat,
The time is right
Brothers and sisters
For a little bit of change
Do you hear the sound
Of distant revolution?
It won't happen overnight,
But you and me,
Can rock the boat a little,
And start to make waves
We're heading for hard times,
You don't see it?

IMAGES

I often project an image,
which makes you feel safe
I keep myself in check,
Showing only a blank face,
Creative activity is kept under wraps,
But frustration fights back
It bursts out of me,
In a crazy disordered fashion,
I regain my composure in time,
And before you can identify,
My little outburst,
My mask is reinstated,
With an inane smile.

SOCIAL HABITS DIE HARD

Command and Obey,
But why is it?
I always assume the latter role,
Its a matter of breaking,
Social upbringing,
I was reared to expect,
Always to be told.

THE SOUND OF YOUR VOICE

Can't we talk one to one
On an equal basis?
After all, we are only,
Flesh and blood!
Do you have to tower above me!
Can't you see that what I'm saying
Makes perfect sense?
Or are you not listening!
Is it the sound,
Of your own voice,
That you like to hear?
It makes you feel superior,
I can see that,
I'll never get through to you!

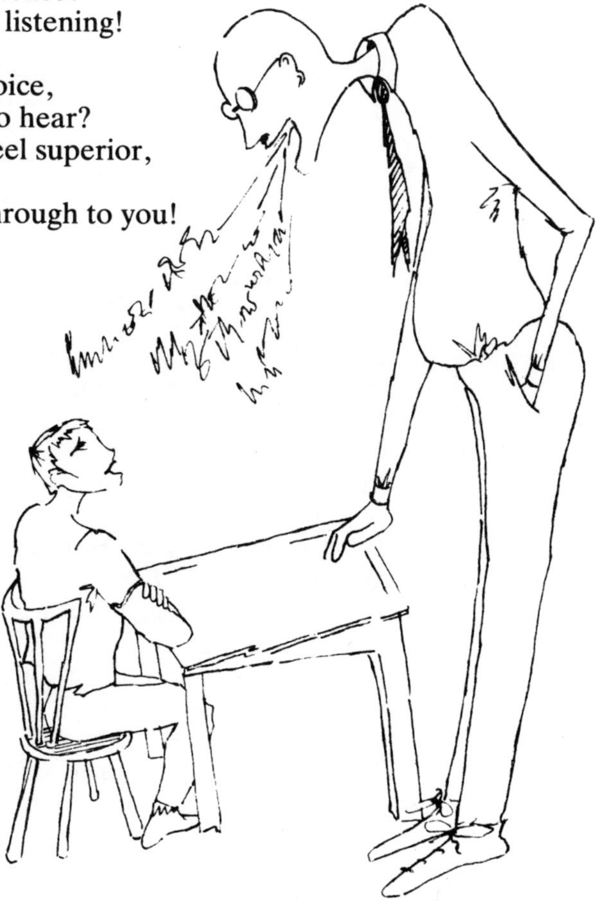

QUEEN OF THE BLUES

Old Father Thames,
Has a story to tell.
About a girl who lived,
Down Kilburn Way.
The pressure of living,
Made her throw her life away.
She could play guitar,
And sing the blues. . . .
But like most blues singers,
She was born to lose.
I wish she was alive today,
To tell me off,
For writing that last statement.

IS LIFE SO BAD?

Life is threatening to strangle me.
Every knock at my pride chokes me
But I haven't got the courage,
To finish off the job,
People tell me life can't be,
So bad and depressing,
But I wake up every morning,
Wishing I wasn't here.
I turn up my Reggae music,
Hoping it'll put me in a
Better frame of mind.
And it does for a time.
But what happens when the music stops?
That when the pressures starts to drop,
On me!

SILENTLY SCREAMING

Silently screaming,
Your silence says more,
Than words ever can.
A silent code full of meaning,
I *know* what you're feeling,
I've been there before
And I want to protect you
From all that's going down,
Don't make a sound,
Because they'll hear you,
And they'll jeer at you,
For being so sensitive,
Don't look around,
Because they'll see,
That you've noticed
There's something wrong.

PARANOIA

Living in a large asylum,
Where television acts as,
The universal anaesthetic,
If you show signs of,
Cracking under the strain,
They call you a misfit,
Strange or insane.

PULSELESS

An open heart,
Cut in two,
One part is false,
One part is true,
But which side are we on?
Can we crossover?
Is there a barrier?
There's two sides to every story
And we use one,
Against the other,
In order to gain power,
And determine,
Who is the slave,
And who is the master,
Its called structured
Society.

GREY FORCES

Brainwashing starts in the morning,
With the arrival of the sun,
It goes on till the little white dot,
Fades into dark grey glass,
1984 is just around the corner,
Maggie's trying for a fascist state,
You accept, you accept, you accept.
And won't even see it,
Till its dangerously too late.

CREATIVE MIND

The past is dead,
You can't resurrect it,
You can't cling onto something,
Unobtainable
Go home and create something
Entirely new!